8 Step Marking Plan

Contents

----

1. Define Your Target Market

2. Set Your Goals:

3. Develop Your Unique Value Proposition

4. How To Create a Content Calendar:

5. How to Leverage Social Media:

6. How to Build an Email List:

7. How to Offer Special Promotions

8. How to Monitor Your Results

By following these steps, you can create a 30-day marketing plan to sell your Product online and drive business growth.

Chapter One

Defining your target market is an essential step in creating an effective marketing strategy. Here are the steps you can follow to define your target market:

1. Analyze Your Product or Service: Start by analyzing your product or service to determine its unique features and benefits. Consider what problem it solves or what needs it fulfills.
2. Identify the Demographics: Identify the demographic characteristics of the people who are most likely to benefit from your product or service. This may include age, gender, income, education, and location.
3. Analyze Your Competition: Research your competition to see who they are targeting and how they are positioning their products or services. This will help you identify gaps in the market and find opportunities to differentiate yourself.
4. Conduct Market Research: Conduct surveys or focus groups with potential

customers to get feedback on your product or service. This will help you identify their needs, preferences, and pain points.

5. Develop Buyer Personas: Develop detailed profiles of your ideal customers based on their demographic characteristics, behaviors, and motivations. This will help you create targeted marketing messages that resonate with them.

6. Refine Your Target Market: Based on your research, refine your target market to a specific group of people who are most likely to purchase your product or service. This will help you tailor your marketing efforts to reach them more effectively.

By following these steps, you can define your target market and create a marketing strategy that resonates with your ideal customers.

Define your Target Market

NOTES

NOTES

NOTES

Chapter Two

Setting marketing goals is a crucial step in creating an effective marketing plan. Here are the steps you can follow to set your marketing goals:

1. Define Your Business Objectives: Start by defining your overall business objectives. What do you want to achieve in the next 6-12 months? Your marketing goals should align with your business objectives.

2. Identify Key Performance Indicators (KPIs): Identify the KPIs that are most relevant to your business objectives. These may include website traffic, lead generation, sales revenue, customer acquisition cost, or customer lifetime value.

3. Set Specific, Measurable, and Realistic Goals: Your marketing goals should be specific, measurable, and realistic. For

example, "Increase website traffic by 25% in the next 30 days" is a specific and measurable goal that is also realistic.

4. Determine Your Timeline: Set a timeline for achieving your marketing goals. This will help you stay focused and motivated. For example, you may set a goal to achieve a certain number of leads or sales within the next 30 days.

5. Assign Responsibilities: Assign responsibilities for achieving your marketing goals to specific team members or departments. This will help ensure that everyone is working towards the same objectives.

6. Monitor Your Progress: Monitor your progress towards achieving your marketing goals on a regular basis. This will help you identify areas where you need to make adjustments or improvements.

By following these steps, you can set clear and actionable marketing goals that align with your business objectives and help you achieve your desired results

Marketing Goals

NOTES

NOTES

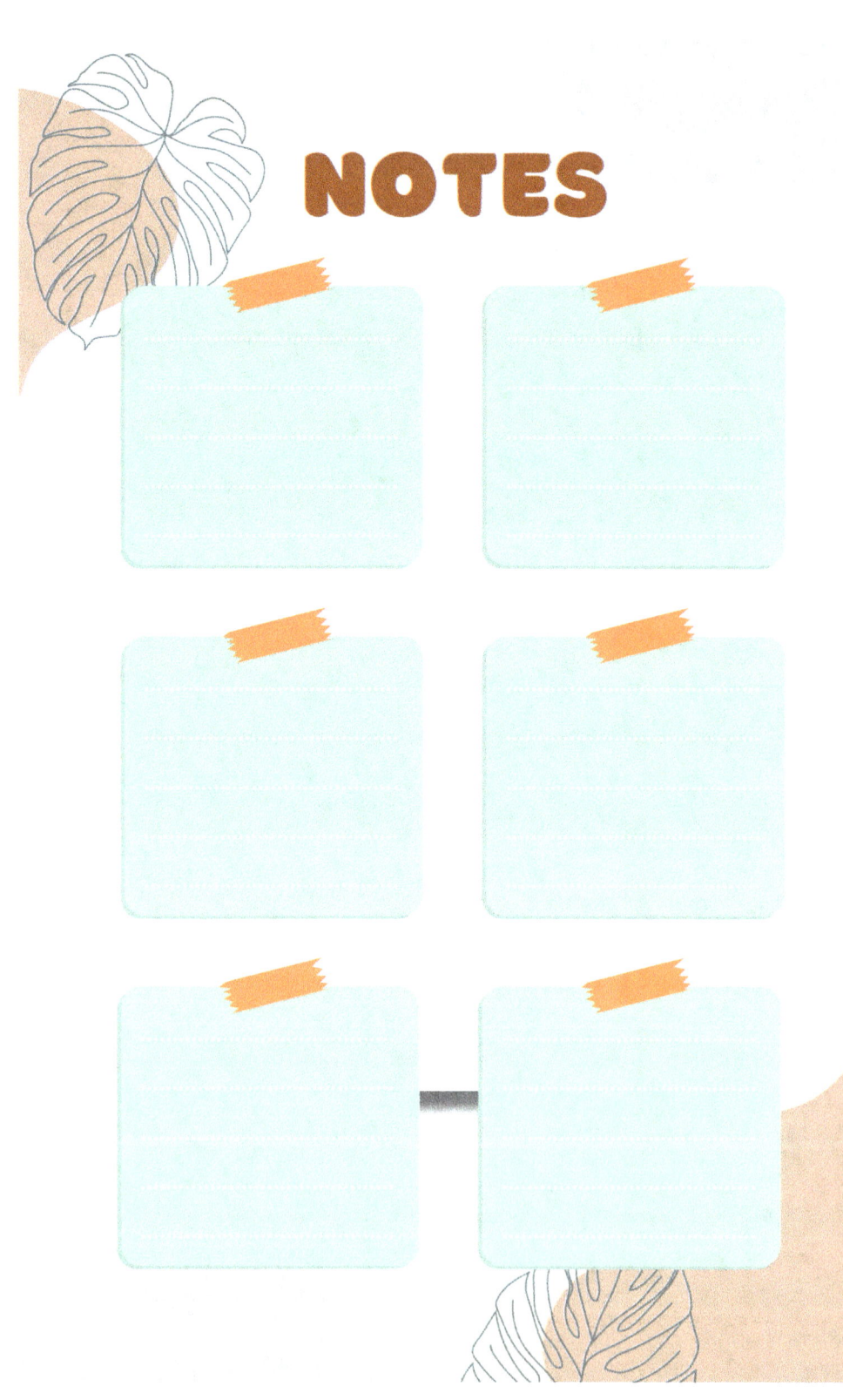

NOTES

NOTES

Chapter Three

Developing a unique value proposition (UVP) is essential in distinguishing your business from competitors and communicating your value to your target market. Here are the steps to follow to develop your UVP:

1. Identify Your Target Audience: Start by identifying your target audience and understanding their needs, wants, and pain points. Consider what problem your product or service solves for them.
2. Analyze Your Competitors: Analyze your competitors' offerings and identify what sets you apart from them. Look for gaps in the market and opportunities to differentiate yourself.
3. Identify Your Unique Benefits: Identify the unique benefits that your product or service provides to your target audience. These may include features, benefits, or outcomes that are different from what your competitors offer.

4. Craft a Compelling Statement: Use the information you have gathered to craft a compelling UVP statement that communicates your unique value to your target audience. Your UVP should be clear, concise, and memorable.
5. Test and Refine Your UVP: Test your UVP with your target audience and gather feedback. Use this feedback to refine your UVP and make it more effective.

Examples of UVP statements include:

- "We provide eco-friendly and affordable cleaning products that are safe for your family and the environment."
- "Our online coaching program helps busy professionals achieve their fitness goals in just 30 minutes a day."
- "Our handmade jewelry is unique and personalized, making every piece one-of-a-kind and special to the wearer."

By following these steps, you can develop a compelling UVP that communicates your unique value to your target audience and helps you stand out from your competitor

NOTES

NOTES

NOTES

NOTES

Chapter Four

Creating a content calendar is an effective way to plan and organize your content marketing strategy. Here are the steps you can follow to create a content calendar:

1. Identify Your Goals: Start by identifying your content marketing goals. What do you want to achieve with your content? This will help you determine the type of content you need to create and the topics you should focus on.
2. Determine Your Target Audience: Determine who your target audience is and what type of content they are interested in. This will help you create content that resonates with them.
3. Choose Your Channels: Choose the channels you will use to distribute your content, such as your website, social media, email, or blog.
4. Brainstorm Content Ideas: Brainstorm content ideas that align with your goals

and are relevant to your target audience. Use keyword research and competitor analysis to find popular topics in your industry.

5. Organize Your Ideas: Organize your content ideas into a calendar format, such as a spreadsheet or online tool. Assign each idea a date and channel for distribution.

6. Create Your Content: Create your content based on the ideas and dates outlined in your content calendar. Make sure your content is high-quality and provides value to your target audience.

7. Track Your Results: Track your results to see what type of content is resonating with your audience and adjust your content calendar as needed.

Here are some tips for creating an effective content calendar:

- Keep it flexible: Leave room for new content ideas and adjustments to your schedule.

- Use visuals: Add visuals to your content calendar to make it more engaging and easier to read.
- Plan ahead: Plan your content at least a month in advance to give yourself enough time to create high-quality content.
- Set realistic goals: Set realistic goals for your content and adjust them based on your results.

By following these steps, you can create a content calendar that helps you achieve your content marketing goals and provides value to your target audience.

Content Calendar

NOTES

NOTES

NOTES

NOTES

Chapter Five

Leveraging social media is an effective way to reach and engage with your target audience. Here are the steps you can follow to leverage social media:

1. Identify Your Target Audience: Start by identifying your target audience and where they spend their time on social media. This will help you determine which platforms to focus on and the type of content to create.
2. Choose Your Platforms: Choose the social media platforms that are most relevant to your target audience and business goals. Some popular options include Facebook, Instagram, Twitter, LinkedIn, and TikTok.
3. Develop a Content Strategy: Develop a content strategy that aligns with your business goals and target audience. Your content should be valuable, engaging, and shareable. Consider using

a mix of formats, such as images, videos, and stories.

4. Engage with Your Audience: Engage with your audience by responding to comments, messages, and reviews. This will help build trust and loyalty with your followers.

5. Utilize Paid Advertising: Utilize paid advertising options on social media platforms to reach a wider audience and increase engagement. Options include sponsored posts, ads, and promoted content.

6. Monitor Your Analytics: Monitor your social media analytics to track your progress and adjust your strategy as needed. Key metrics to track include engagement, reach, clicks, and conversions.

7. Stay Up-to-Date with Trends: Stay up-to-date with the latest social media trends and changes to algorithms to ensure your content is optimized for success.

Here are some tips for leveraging social media effectively:

- Be authentic: Be authentic and transparent in your social media presence to build trust with your audience.
- Post regularly: Post regularly and consistently to keep your audience engaged and interested.
- Use visuals: Use visuals, such as images and videos, to make your content more engaging and shareable.
- Collaborate with influencers: Collaborate with influencers in your industry to reach a wider audience and increase brand awareness.

By following these steps and tips, you can effectively leverage social media to reach and engage with your target audience and achieve your business goals.

Social Media

NOTES

NOTES

NOTES

NOTES

Chapter Six

Building an email list is an important aspect of email marketing and can help you stay in touch with your target audience, promote your products or services, and drive conversions. Here are some steps you can follow to build an email list:

1. Choose an Email Marketing Service: Choose an email marketing service provider that fits your budget and business needs. Some popular options include Mailchimp, Constant Contact, and AWeber.
2. Create a Lead Magnet: Create a lead magnet, such as a free ebook, checklist, or webinar, that provides value to your target audience and encourages them to sign up for your email list.
3. Add Opt-In Forms to Your Website: Add opt-in forms to your website, such as pop-ups, slide-ins, or forms in the

sidebar or footer, to encourage visitors to sign up for your email list.

4. Offer Incentives: Offer incentives, such as a discount or exclusive content, to those who sign up for your email list to further encourage sign-ups.
5. Promote Your Email List: Promote your email list on social media, through guest blogging, and in other marketing channels to reach a wider audience.
6. Segment Your List: Segment your email list based on demographics, interests, and behavior to send targeted and personalized emails that resonate with your subscribers.
7. Test and Optimize: Test and optimize your email list building strategy to improve your sign-up rates and ensure your emails are getting delivered and opened.

Here are some tips for building an effective email list:

- Focus on Quality: Focus on quality subscribers who are interested in your products or services, rather than quantity.

- Be Transparent: Be transparent about what subscribers can expect to receive from your emails and how often they will receive them.
- Use Clear and Compelling Copy: Use clear and compelling copy in your opt-in forms and lead magnets to encourage sign-ups.
- Make it Easy to Unsubscribe: Make it easy for subscribers to unsubscribe from your emails to avoid damaging your reputation and getting marked as spam.

By following these steps and tips, you can build an effective email list that helps you stay in touch with your target audience and drive business results

Chapter Seven

Offering special promotions is a great way to incentivize customers to make a purchase, boost sales, and increase customer loyalty. Here are some steps you can follow to create special promotions:

1. Define Your Goals: Define your goals for the promotion, such as increasing sales or attracting new customers.
2. Determine Your Promotion Type: Determine the type of promotion that fits your goals and budget. Common types include discounts, free gifts with purchase, limited-time offers, and referral programs.
3. Set the Terms and Conditions: Set the terms and conditions for your promotion, including the duration, discount amount, and eligibility criteria.
4. Create Promotional Materials: Create promotional materials, such as social media posts, email campaigns, and website banners, to promote your special offer.

5. Launch Your Promotion: Launch your promotion and communicate it to your target audience through multiple marketing channels.
6. Track Results: Track the results of your promotion to see if you achieved your goals and adjust your strategy as needed.
7. Follow Up with Customers: Follow up with customers who participated in the promotion to thank them and encourage future purchases.

Here are some tips for creating effective special promotions:

- Make it Limited-Time: Create a sense of urgency by making your promotion limited-time only.
- Be Clear: Clearly communicate the terms and conditions of your promotion to avoid confusion and ensure customer satisfaction.
- Offer Value: Ensure that your promotion offers real value to customers to encourage them to make a purchase.

- Target Your Audience: Target your promotion to your ideal customers to maximize its impact.

By following these steps and tips, you can create effective special promotions that drive sales and customer loyalty

NOTES

NOTES

NOTES

NOTES

Chapter Eight

Monitoring your marketing results is important to ensure that you are achieving your goals and to identify areas for improvement. Here are some steps you can follow to monitor your marketing results:

1. Define Your Metrics: Define the metrics that you will use to measure the success of your marketing efforts. Some common metrics include website traffic, leads generated, conversion rates, social media engagement, and email open and click-through rates.

2. Use Analytics Tools: Use analytics tools, such as Google Analytics, social media analytics, and email marketing software, to track your metrics and monitor your marketing results.

3. Analyze Your Data: Analyze your data regularly to identify trends, patterns, and areas for improvement. Use this data to make informed decisions and adjust your marketing strategy as needed.

4. Set Benchmarks: Set benchmarks for your metrics to help you track your progress over time and compare your results to industry standards.
5. Create Reports: Create regular reports that summarize your marketing results and provide insights into your performance. Use these reports to communicate your results to stakeholders and make data-driven decisions.
6. Test and Experiment: Test and experiment with different marketing tactics and strategies to see what works best for your business. Use A/B testing and other experimentation techniques to refine your approach and improve your results.
7. Continuously Improve: Continuously improve your marketing strategy based on your results and feedback from your audience. Stay up-to-date with industry trends and best practices to stay ahead of the competition.

By following these steps, you can monitor your marketing results effectively and make data-driven decisions that help you achieve your business goals.

NOTES

NOTES

NOTES

NOTES

Why Marketing your business is extremely important :

1. Builds Brand Awareness: Marketing helps you build brand awareness and make your business known to potential customers. By consistently promoting your brand through various channels, you can increase the chances of people recognizing and remembering your business.

2. Drives Sales: Effective marketing can help you drive sales by attracting new customers, retaining existing ones, and encouraging repeat purchases. By targeting the right audience with the right message, you can increase your chances of converting leads into paying customers.

3. Increases Customer Loyalty: By staying in touch with your customers through marketing channels such as email and social media, you can keep them engaged and informed about your business. This helps build customer loyalty and encourages repeat business.

4. Helps You Stand Out: Marketing helps you differentiate your business from your competitors and highlight your unique selling proposition. This can help you stand out in a crowded market and increase your chances of attracting customers.
5. Supports Business Growth: Effective marketing can support business growth by helping you reach new markets, expand your customer base, and increase revenue.

In summary, marketing is essential for building brand awareness, driving sales, increasing customer loyalty, standing out from competitors, and supporting business growth. By investing in marketing efforts, you can increase your chances of success and build a strong, sustainable business.

NOTES

NOTES

NOTES

NOTES

NOTES

NOTES

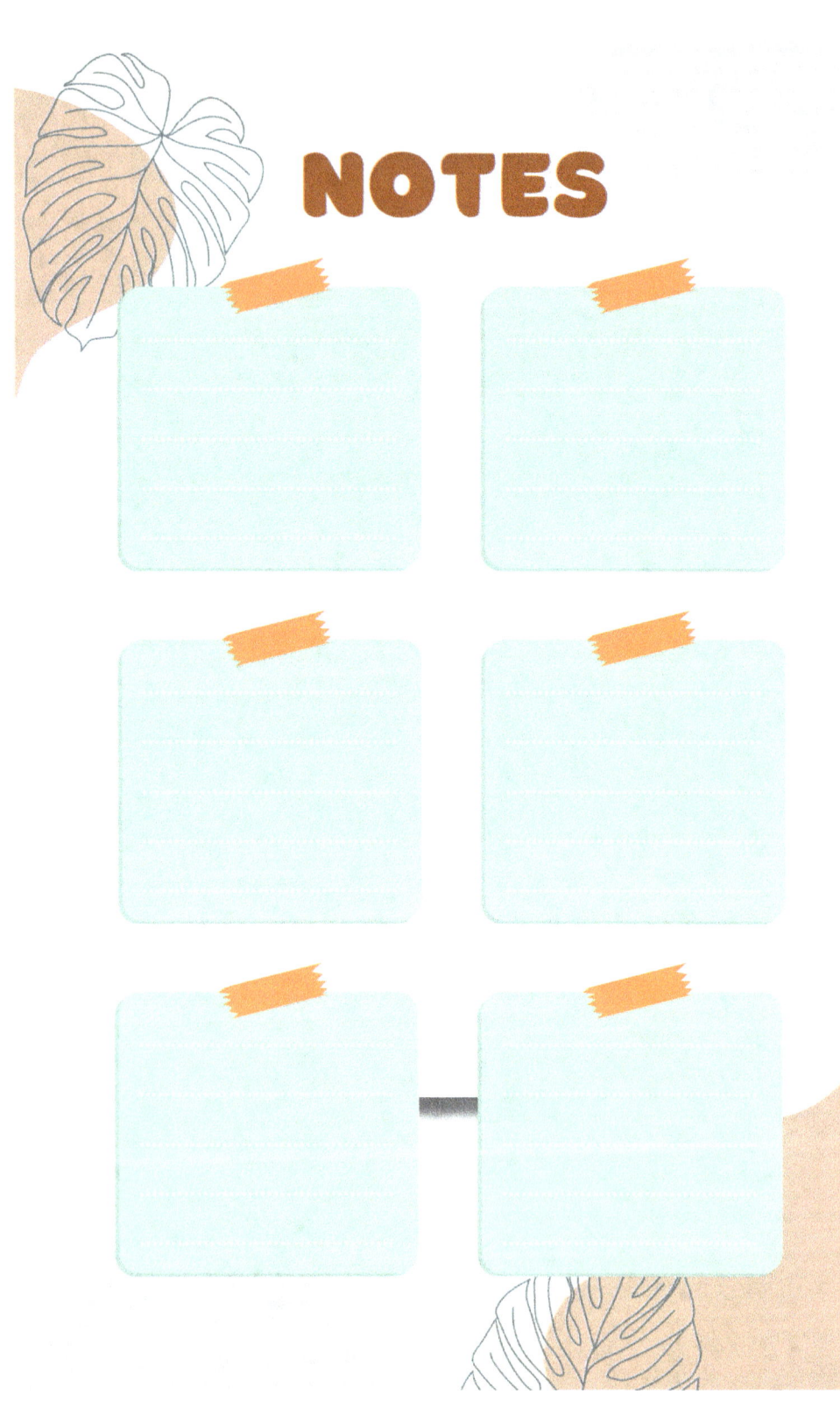

NOTES

NOTES

NOTES

NOTES

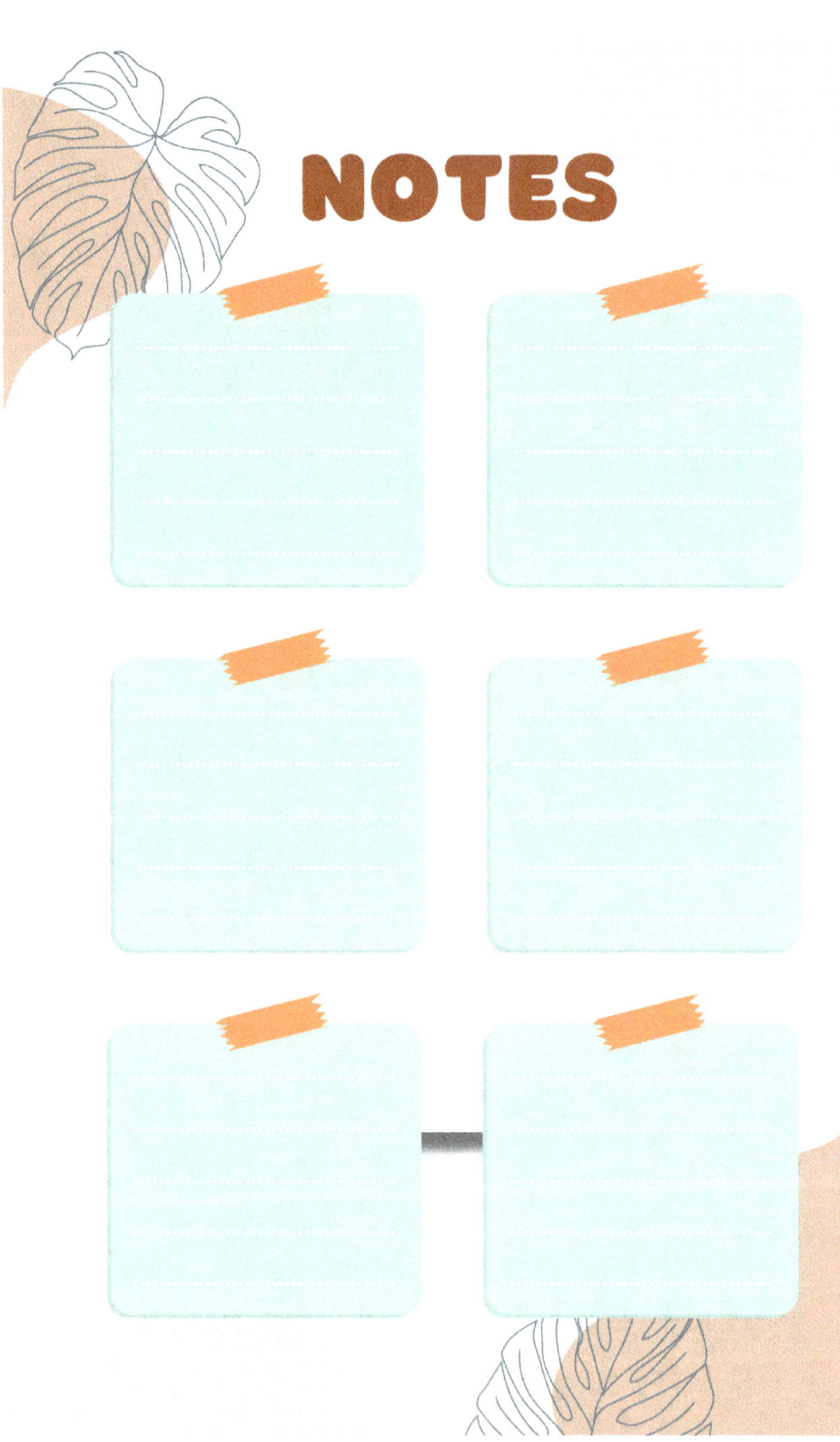

Endless good now comes to you in endless ways

-Shinn-